WHAT SELF-ESTEEM

TRAINING DOES YOUR CHILD

NEED TODAY?

JANA CAPRI
CHARAN DÍAZ

WHAT SELF-ESTEEM TRAINING DOES YOUR CHILD NEED TODAY?

(Sowing self-esteem in the present so your child can have confidence in the future)

2 IN 1: AN EXERCISE AND COLORING BOOK

Urano
publishing

Argentina - Chile - Colombia - Spain
USA - Mexico - Peru - Uruguay

© 2023 by Jana Capri & Charan Díaz

© 2023 by Urano Publishing, an imprint of Urano World USA, Inc

8871 SW 129th Terrace Miami FL 33176 USA

Urano
publishing

Illustrations by Yulia Valerevna Bagdasarova

Cover art and design by Luis Tinoco

Cover copyright © Urano Publishing, an imprint of Urano World USA, Inc

The first edition of this book was published in November 2023

This English language edition published by special arrangement with Montse Cortazar Literary Agency (www.montsecortazar.com)

ISBN: 978-1-953027-22-1

E-ISBN: 978-1-953027-23-8

Printed in Spain

Library of Cataloging-in-Publication Data

Capri, Jana & Díaz, Charan

1. Self-help   2. Child Development

What Self-Esteem Training Does Your Child Need Today?

Dedicated to all the children who are now parents and believe that life is better with strong self-esteem.

Especially dedicated to Anaïs Díaz A., Albert García V., Monika Gorgon, and Javier Auñón A.

To our parents—bottomless pits of love.

Editor's note: This book is aimed at children, but at times will require the help of an adult (father, mother, grandfather, grand-mother, teacher, etc.). We aim to use language that is as inclusive as possible. On occasion we use gender-neutral terms, such as "child", "adult", "they", or more specific terms, such as "Mom and Dad", for ease of reading. We do not intend for these language choices to be disrespectful to the reader in any way. Thank you very much for your understanding.

INTRODUCTION

If we went out into the street to conduct a survey to identify the strongest hope that parents have for their children, they would most likely tell us that they wish for happiness and good health.

There is no need to perform an in-depth analysis of these two wishes to realize they are in fact referring to the same thing—HEALTH, both physical and mental.

The goal of this book is to provide practical tools to increase SELF-ESTEEM and CONFIDENCE during childhood and, as a result, contribute to the healthy development of children's mental health, making them happier in the long term.

It does not matter if we are 7 or 77 years old, to successfully solve problems in life, make good decisions, and be happy, it is necessary to maintain a good level of self-esteem and to take care of our own well-being. Our parents, guardians, and role models have taught us many things, but there is still a very clear gap when it comes to learning to love and value ourselves, and to have confidence, in ourselves, in others, and in life.

Like our first book on this topic, *The Oracle Book of Self-esteem and Confidence,* which is aimed at young people and adults, this book provides highly practical exercises and gets straight to the point. Fun new elements, only present in this children's version, are the drawings and exercises, which make reading much more entertaining and interactive.

The book contains 32 exercises that will guide children between the ages of 7 and 13 towards feeling better about themselves. The exercises have been designed so that children learn to:

- Identify their strengths and remain conscious of them.
- See the positive side of all situations.
- Establish healthy relationships.
- Communicate with confidence.
- Create self-care habits.
- Better understand their emotions.
- Manage failures and mistakes with self-esteem.
- Practice gratitude.

HOW TO USE THIS BOOK

How the exercises in this book are structured

1. Section for the child
2. Instructions for the adult who is working with the child on the exercise
3. The goal of the exercise
4. Page to fill in or a coloring page (on the opposite page)

Support and adaptation of the exercise

To get the most out of the exercises in this book, it is important that an adult work with the child, to help them understand and complete the activities.

The exercises have been designed for children between the ages of 7 and 13. Nonetheless, depending on the age and the level of maturity of the child, sometimes it may be best to adapt the materials. For example, in exercise 17, MY

SUPERHERO, a young child may think of a hero from an animated movie but an older child may think of their idol, a real person that they admire.

If the exercise comes with a drawing, the adult can help the child understand how the drawing is related to the activity. After the activity, the child is free to color the drawing on their own, without the help of an adult.

Topics and purpose of the exercises

As you can see in the table of contents, we have grouped the activities into 5 key topics:

- SELF-KNOWLEDGE AND SELF-LOVE
- GRATITUDE, ENTHUSIASM AND OPTIMISM
- ROLE MODELS AND GOOD INFLUENCES
- ASSERTIVENESS AND RELATIONSHIPS
- CONFIDENCE, OVERCOMING ADVERSITY, AND RE-SILIENCE

Some exercises don't require any particular context and it is beneficial to repeat them frequently. Regular practice of these exercises will help to boost self-esteem and confidence.

These "routine" exercises are marked with a square symbol, ■, and the usefulness of these exercises is increased through repetition.

Other exercises respond to a specific context or situation and help the child to improve or solve a problem, doubt, or discomfort. We call these types of exercises "circumstantial" and they are marked with a star symbol. ★

Many exercises fit in both categories. In these cases, they are marked as "routine/circumstantial." ■ ★

In the Exercise Table (p. 147), you can find a list of all the exercises, specifying the type of exercise and tips for their use. The table can be used as a cheat sheet to help choose an exercise that is tailored to the child's needs.

At the end of the book, we have included a small prize for the child. After the last exercise, there are pages with **copies** of the drawings and the exercises that can be filled in. These can be:

- filled in and colored once again
- copied and saved for the future
- cut out and hung on the wall, door, desk, or used for whatever the child feels like doing!

RECOMMENDATION: We recommend using colored pencils to color in the drawings.

SELF-KNOWLEDGE
AND SELF-LOVE

1

■

I AM BRAVE

Think of a situation in which you have been brave:

This week;
This year;
Throughout your life.

How did being brave help you?
What did you feel when you were brave?

Instructions for parents: Help your child to remember all their moments of bravery, and to understand that they can overcome fear and achieve many great things in life.

Goal: This exercise helps a child to focus on moments where they have shown courage and bravery. By being conscious of these moments, the child can perceive themself as having the strength and resources needed to overcome difficulties, as well as to gain confidence in their ability to overcome challenges by building resilience.

2

■ ★

A TIGER DOESN'T WANT

TO HAVE WINGS

Imagine a tiger saying, "I want to have wings and buzz
like a fly!"
Or a sheep saying, "I wish I could sing as well as
a mockingbird!"
Or a fish saying, "Why don't I have legs to be able
to run like a gazelle?"

Animals don't think like that. A tiger doesn't want to be
a fly and a sheep doesn't want to be a mockingbird.
Each animal is happy with the body and abilities that
nature has gifted them.

What has nature gifted you?
Remember, when you try to be like others, you are
like a tiger that wants to fly or a
fish that wants to walk.

Instructions for parents: If your child is envious of the body,
face, talent, age, etc., of another person, you can use this
example of animals, emphasizing the fact that we should be

satisfied with what we have and that we should not chase after traits that we lack.

Goal: The child learns to avoid comparing themself in a way that is unconstructive, and to love themself just the way they are, appreciating what makes them unique.

WHAT HAVE I LEARNED?

My new KNOWLEDGE is...

_____

_____

_____

_____

_____

My new ABILITIES are...

_____

_____

_____

_____

_____

From my EXPERIENCE, I learned that...

_____

_____

_____

_____

_____

3

■

I AM ALWAYS LEARNING

What did you learn this month/year?

It can be:

- New KNOWLEDGE (example, now I know how to count to twenty in a foreign language).

- New ABILITIES (example, I learned to swim).

- New learning that comes from EXPERIENCE (example, I learned that if I go to sleep early, I will have more energy in the morning).

How do you feel about what you've learned?

Instructions for parents: Help your child to value their ability to learn. You will enable them to see that they are a good student of life. They will come to understand that, with a little bit of learning, perseverance, and patience, they can achieve many things.

Goal: Remind, reinforce, and help your child to appreciate what they learned (no matter how minor it may seem). This is essential to increase the self-esteem and confidence of the child. In this way, the child will understand that if they were able to learn something in the past, they'll also be able to learn more significant things in the future.

4

★

I'M AFRAID OF...

Four steps to confront fears:

1. What are you afraid of?
2. Why are you afraid of it?
3. Who can you ask for help?
4. What can you do to feel better, right here and now?

Instructions for parents: In Step 2, you must get to the bottom of the issue. Sometimes it's necessary to ask more than once about the "why" hidden behind a particular issue. For example, if the child is afraid of an exam, it is important to discover what is behind that fear. Is it fear of their parents' reaction? Fear of being teased in class if they fail?

In Step 3, you remind your child that they can ask for help and receive support in all situations in life, but they should be aware of whom to ask for help. We are not alone and we can get support if we ask for it. And it's smart to do so whenever necessary.

In Step 4, the child finds a way to reduce their own fear and parents can contribute ideas.

Example: Sometimes small children fear going to sleep because of the monster under the bed. A child might think that the monster can hurt them or take them away. The child might believe they will be better off in their parent's bed. In this situation, a parent can help the child to understand that monsters don't exist, that the parent is close and will hear them if they call out, or that they can say a prayer or recite positive words of affirmation.

Goal: Aim to get to the bottom of what is driving your child's fear to reduce its strength. Show your child that they have your support and that you will not allow anything to harm them. By discovering ways to handle their fears, the child can build confidence in themselves, in others, and in life.

MY SUPERPOWER

My SUPERPOWER is…

_____

_____

_____

_____

_____

I use this SUPERPOWER when…

_____

_____

_____

_____

_____

The best thing about my SUPERPOWER is…

_____

_____

_____

_____

_____

5

◼

MY SUPERPOWER

What do you like about yourself? What are you good at?

Did you know that "what you like about yourself" is a superpower?

(Note that this superpower should not be something superficial or related to physical appearance, and should be a talent or strength of the child).

Instructions for parents: Help your child to identify a positive personality trait or characteristic and turn it into a superpower for your son or daughter. After that, the child should think of a situation in which they used their superpower in the past, and how it can help them in the future. To make it more interactive, you can share your superpower too, and discuss it with your child.

Example: If the child likes to play soccer, and they value this in themselves. The adult can identify how important it is to not give up on soccer (i.e., perseverance). Together they can re-member a past situation in which, thanks to perseverance, a problem or challenge was overcome (for example, success-fully completing a class assignment).

Goal: The child should learn to discover new things about themself and recognize personality traits that encourage their self-esteem and confidence. By calling them a "superpower", the child will connect themself with the idea of superheroes, which should make them feel stronger and more special.

THE EMOTIONS GAME

HAPPY

SCARED

GRATEFUL

WORRIED

EXCITED

ANGRY

KIND

BORED

FRUSTRATED

CONFUSED

STRESSED

CALM

LONELY

FEELING INJUSTICE

ANXIOUS

CONFIDENT

GUILTY

ENVIOUS

BRAVE

CHEERFUL

CURIOUS

ASHAMED

SAD

GLAD

THRILLED

6

■ ★

THE EMOTIONS GAME

What emotion are you feeling right now?
For inspiration, have a look at the previous page.
Why do you feel like this? In which part of the body do
you notice it?

Do you want to keep that emotion, or would you prefer
to swap it for another? If you prefer to swap it, then
think:

How does a child act when they're feeling sad, mad, glad, or
joyous?

Instructions for parents: With your child, identify the strongest emotion they feel at the moment, this week, when they do an activity, when they're with a particular person, etc., and help them to understand why they might feel that way.

If it is a negative emotion, play the game of choosing a good emotion and think about what they could do or think to feel that emotion. The child can write the emotion that they would like to feel on a large piece of paper; have them color the letters, add drawings, etc. After that, they can hang the page in a visible place or put it in their pocket as a reminder.

Example: A girl is bored because no one wants to play with her. How would she prefer to feel? Happy. The girl thinks of ideas for how to feel happy and, with the adult, comes up with a plan. The girl is given the challenge to find a game that she is excited about and can play alone. After doing this, the adult plays another game with her, this time a game for two people.

Goal: With this exercise, the child practices how to be more conscious of their emotional state and moods. They learn to understand why they feel what they feel, and how to choose a more enjoyable emotion (with a little creativity and dedication).

7

■ ★

WHAT DO I SEE IN THE MIRROR?

Stand in front of a mirror. Look at your body and face,
and point to every part of your body, saying:
"Nobody has a… like me".

*Example: Nobody has a nose like mine; nobody has
eyes like mine; nobody has hands like mine.*

See? Your body is unique. Nobody has a body like
yours.

Now do the same exercise again but this time say:
"I like the hair that I have because…; I like my arms
because…; I like…»

Instructions for parents: Help your child to feel positive
about their own body, emphasizing the fact that all faces and
bodies are unique, and that all are worthy of being loved and
pampered. To make the activity more entertaining, you can
also do this exercise.

Goal: This exercise helps the child to generate a more positive image of their own body and to avoid comparing themselves to others. This should help them to develop a healthy level of self-esteem regarding their body.

THE POWER OF MY HABITS

My GOOD habits are…

_____
_____
_____
_____
_____

My BAD habits are…

_____
_____
_____
_____
_____

What other good habits could I include in my list and practice?
Today, I can switch a bad habit for a good one, which one will
it be?

_____
_____
_____
_____
_____

8

■

THE POWER OF MY HABITS

What are your habits? What things do you do,
and repeat, every day?

Write your good and bad habits down on the previous
page.

*Example: Listening to a story or reading before going
to sleep; biting your nails; making your bed every
morning; playing video games.*

GOOD HABITS: How do these habits help you? Why are they
good? What other good habits can you include in your list and
put into practice?

BAD HABITS: How can you stop doing them? Can you substitute a bad habit with a good one?

Instructions for parents: Little children will need your help to
identify habits. Allow the child to decide if these habits are
good or bad and why. Develop a plan for bad habits (for example, the challenge might be for the child to not bite their
nails for 3 days in a row, and if they succeed they'll receive a
prize). With your child, reflect on what new habits could be

introduced and discuss their advantages. The child can then decide which of these good habits they'd like to put into practice over the next 7 days. After this period, discuss with the child how they found the experience of putting these habits into practice and what benefits they have felt.

Goal: To analyze the habits of the child and introduce new self-care habits that reinforce their self-esteem.

9

★

I AM CAPABLE

Think of one thing you think you are not capable
of doing.
Why aren't you able to do or achieve it?
What would make you feel capable of doing it?
Try two more examples.

Instructions for parents: Identify what is behind the lack of
confidence in your child.

1. Behind many "I'm not able to" or "I can't" is an "I don't
   want to", especially when it comes to chores that a child
   doesn't feel like doing. It's important that the child understand that it's not about a lack of ability, but rather a
   lack of will.
2. The child may need more practice or support to feel
   capable of accomplishing a chore, challenge, etc.
   What does the child need to feel more capable?
3. If the child is comparing themselves with someone
   more advanced than them (in age, experience, etc.)
   and they feel paralyzed, it's important to explain to
   them that the only fair comparison is with themself and
   their own progress. If the child practices, they'll improve
   and will feel more capable than before.

4. The child may be too demanding of themself and feel incapable of doing something, when in fact, they are able to. Give the child examples of what they achieved in the past and encourage them to see their abilities in a more positive light.

Goal: Understand the situations in which the child sees themself as incapable and replace self-destructive beliefs with more constructive ones.

MY STRENGTHS

Strengths that I see in me…

_____

_____

_____

_____

_____

Strengths that OTHERS see in me…

_____

_____

_____

_____

_____

My 3 FAVORITE strengths are…

Strength 1   _____

_____

Strength 2   _____

_____

Strength 3   _____

_____

10

■

MY STRENGTHS

What are you good at? What are your strengths?
What do you like about yourself?
Write your strengths down on the previous page.

Ask your parents, siblings, other family members,
friends, or teachers to identify your strengths. Write
down those strengths too.

Of all the strengths listed, choose the 3 that you like
the most. Highlight and remember them.

Instructions for parents: It's a good idea to copy the previous
page, fill it in, and hang it up in a visible place. When the child
has a bad day, remembering their list of strengths can cheer
them up. You can also check the list and think about how to
reinforce your child's talents and self-esteem even more.

Example 1 (talent): She like to sing and others think that she
sings well. Sign her up for singing lessons.

Example 2 (personality): A boy likes the fact that he's respon-
sible and that he can be trusted. So, think of activities that

reinforce the boy's sense of responsibility, such as caring for a pet, going out to shop on his own, etc. (adapt the activity to the age of the child).

Goal: Remembering one's strengths will help the child to reinforce their self-esteem and be conscious that they have talents, abilities, and characteristics that others appreciate about them.

11

■ ★

I AM ME

Step 1:

Do you know someone that is better than you at something (e.g., is that person smarter, do they have more friends, are they better at a sport or subject in class)?

How does that make you feel?
Would you like to be liked by that person?

Step 2:

Now, think of an activity in which you are better than that person. (How to make your child feel more confident).

Step 3:

You are unique. Nobody is like you.
The fact that someone knows how to do something better than you does not mean that they are better than you. Don't compare yourself to others, we all have our strengths.

Instructions for parents: If your child compares themself frequently to others, go directly to step 2.

Goal: To make it clear that we are all, both, talented and less skilled at different things and that we shouldn't compare ourselves to others. For example, if Silvia knows how to draw better than Nicholas, Silvia may have practiced more. Nicholas may know how to sing better because he practiced that instead.

GRATITUDE, ENTHUSIASM, AND OPTIMISM

12

■★

INVISIBLE GIFTS

Tell me 3 things that have gone well today.

Questions that will help stimulate an answer:
Have you seen anything interesting today?
Did you eat anything yummy?
Has anyone told you something nice?
Has anything made you laugh?

What was good about these things?

Instructions for parents: Explain to the child that all the good things that happened to them today are like **invisible gifts.** Gifts are not just toys, dolls, etc. It is also a gift when someone says something nice about us, makes us laugh, or when we take a pretty picture of a flower or pet a dog; every day we receive a lot of invisible gifts. You can share with your child an invisible gift you received today.

Goal: This exercise will help the child to recognize and appreciate good things that are present in daily life that aren't always clearly visible. This activity also helps the child to practice gratitude and should reduce their levels of frustration and anger.

13

■ ★

I CAN TURN IT AROUND!

Is there something that you don't like about yourself? What is positive about it? (Find something good in the bad).

Everything has two sides; you just have to see them. Turn what you don't like around, and you will find something positive.

Examples:

- Do you think you have too few friends? Well, it's better to have a small number of very good friends than a lot of bad friends.
- Do you think you have too few toys? You can learn to have fun and be creative by drawing, singing, and inventing games and stories. What matters is not the toys but rather the ability to play. Even if you don't have many toys, you can still come up with a lot of games.

Instructions for parents: It's preferable for your child to think for themself about the positive side of everything, and when they can't think of anything you can help. The turns will be more memorable and have a greater impact for the child when they're creative and fun!

Goal: The child learns to see that negative things can have a good side or an advantage. This exercise boosts positive thinking, weakens toxic beliefs, and widens one's perspectives and worldview.

MY LIST OF DREAMS

Dream 1: _____

_____

_____

Dream 2: _____

_____

_____

Dream 3: _____

_____

_____

14

█

MY LIST OF DREAMS

What are your dreams?
Write them down on the previous page.

1. When you write down your dream, color in the first star.
2. When you think of a plan to achieve your dream, color in the second star. You're already one step closer to your dream!
3. When your dream **comes true,** it's time to color the third star. Congratulations!

Instructions for parents: It is better that the dreams be achievable in the short term. Realistic and achievable dreams will better motivate a child and will be more tangible.

Example: Going to a theme park or riding a pony are good examples of short-term dreams. A dream that is more difficult to achieve and that is long-term can also be included (e.g., "when I'm older, I want to be an actress"), but make sure that not all the dreams are long-term.

Goal: Dreams help a child to have hope and maintain a positive attitude. A dream coming true reminds them that they can attain special things in life as long as they have a plan to achieve them and practice patience and perseverance.

15

■

WHAT WOULD I DO WITHOUT...?

We all have very nice things in life that we should learn to appreciate, but sometimes we forget about them.

Now, think about all the good things that you have in your life and ask yourself:
What would I do without...? How would I feel without...?
And when you finish, say: "How lucky I am to have...!"

Example: How would you feel without your house, your parents, your room, your friends, or the good food your parents cook?

Instructions for parents: Your child should not be left with the fear of losing something valuable; instead, they should end this exercise with a spirit of gratitude for what they have. That is why it's important to end with a phrase of gratitude, such as "how lucky am I to", "I feel very grateful", or "I have reasons to be happy".

Goal: This is an exercise that reminds a child of all the good things in their life and reinforces gratitude. The child will learn not to take everything for granted and to appreciate the value of everything.

HAPPY HERE AND NOW

These are 5 things that make me happy here and now:

1. _____
2. _____
3. _____
4. _____
5. _____

16

■ ★

HAPPY HERE AND NOW

Think of 5 things that make you happy here and now.

Instructions for parents: Your child will practice being happy with little and recognize all the good things that surround them. You will need to guide them so that the "5 things" are non-material in nature (it makes me happy that the whole family is together right now, that it's sunny, that Mom smiles, etc.).

This is a good exercise for when your child is bored or frustrated. For example, when they're in a waiting room, in the car, or eating at the table, and it can serve as a routine exercise.

To use this exercise regularly, it's a good idea to make a copy of the previous page.

> **Goal:** This exercise helps the child to recognize the good things that are present in their lives, but that have no material value. This activity helps the child to practice gratitude and happiness, and to reduce their level of frustration and anger.

ROLE MODELS AND GOOD INFLUENCES

DRAW YOUR SUPERHERO

MY SUPERHERO IS:

_____

17

★

MY SUPERHERO

Who is your superhero?
(This can be a cartoon hero, the character from a
story, Dad, Mom, or a friend).

Why is that person (or character) your superhero?

Imagine that you're him/her/them.
How do you behave? How do you feel?

Instructions for parents: Think of something that your child struggles with or a situation that causes them discomfort or insecurity. Now ask what their superhero would do in that situation. For example, what posture might their hero adopt with their body? Then, see what the child feels and thinks when they take on this new posture.

Example: Superhero—Spiderman. Why does the child like him? Because he fights bad guys and always wins. Situation that causes discomfort: The child struggles to sleep. Ask what Spiderman would do to sleep. Let the child think of a creative solution that makes sense. If the answer doesn't help, try to come up with another solution together. For example, what body posture would Spiderman adopt to be more relaxed and be able to rest? You must emphasize that Spiderman also needs to sleep to have energy and strength for the next day.

Goal: A child imagines themself with the strength they find in a superhero and uses it to their benefit in any given situation. By accompanying the exercise with gestures and actions, the child also learns to use the relationship between their body and mind in their favor.

18

■ ★

GOOD FRIENDS

Who are your friends?

What does a good friend do or say? Give an example.

What does a bad friend do or say? Give an example.

Are you a good friend? Why?

Instructions for parents: Encourage your child to think of the characteristics or qualities of a good friend and ask if any of their friends have those qualities. Vice versa, let them think of a friend first and then identify if they really are a good friend or not. If parents suspect that the child hangs out with other kids that may negatively influence them, this exercise can open the child's eyes and help them understand that someone is not a good friend just because they pay attention to the child or are fun to spend time with.

Goal: In essence, the qualities of a good friend are the qualities of a good person. With this exercise, the child learns to recognize good people in their environment. At the same time, the child evaluates themself in the role of a friend and identifies the good things that they do or say to others and themself.

DRAW YOUR FAVORITE ANIMAL:

MY FAVORITE ANIMAL IS:

_____

19

★

MY FAVORITE ANIMAL

What is your favorite animal?
Why do you like that animal?

Imagine you're that animal.
What do you do? How do you feel?

Instructions for parents: Think of something that your child struggles with or a situation that causes them discomfort or insecurity. Now ask what their favorite animal would do in that situation.

Example: Favorite Animal—Penguin. Why do you like it? Because the penguin is never alone as he lives with many other penguins who help each other (a clue here is that the child may need an increased support from others). The situation causing discomfort: The "bad" kid from the class. Ask what a penguin (now with the help of his community, that is his family, friends, etc.) would do if the bad kid spoke ill to it, what would they say to the bad kid, and how would their strength help them? Would they seek help from a teacher (or another person), etc.?

Goal: The child imagines themself with the strength they find in their favorite animal and uses it to their benefit in the right situation. The child uses their imagination and creativity to increase resilience in difficult situations.

ASSERTIVENESS
AND RELATIONSHIPS

20

■ ★

TOGETHER WE ACCOMPLISH MORE

A father asked his son to move a huge rock from the road.
The son tried to move it unsuccessfully.
"Impossible!" he explained.
"So," the father asked, "did you use all of your strength?"
And the son answered, "yes."
Then, the father said, "No, you didn't! Because I'm your father. I'm here with you but you still haven't asked me for help!"

When you need to do something difficult, do you ask someone for help? Think about the last time that you asked someone for help and explain how they helped you.

Who can help you this week with something?
A friend? Your parents? Your siblings? A teacher?

Instructions for parents: Encourage your child to think of examples where someone else's help was very useful or even essential.

Goal: The child learns to recognize when it is good to ask for help and comes to understand that more things can be accomplished together than when alone. This is a good exercise for self-sufficient and self-demanding children, because they'll learn that asking for help isn't something shameful and is intelligent (and sometimes inevitable). This activity will also help them to practice assertiveness and develop a healthy degree of self-esteem.

21

■

TODAY I WILL TEACH YOU
SOMETHING

Think of something you know how to do but that your
Mom, Dad, or grandparents don't know how to do.

Your parents and grandparents have taught you many
things, but today you will teach them something. Ask
them when they have time for you to teach them
something and prepare yourself.

Example: You teach them to play a game, to draw something,
to play a melody on an instrument, show them a picture of
your classmates and ask them to memorize their names, etc.

Instructions for parents: If your child can't come up with
anything, help them to discover one ability that they have that
they can teach others. The adults must find some free time
and be willing students in this exercise.

Goal: Having the opportunity to teach an adult something will increase a child's confidence in their skills and in their ability to share something positive, original, or useful with another person. This exercise also helps to practice assertiveness because the child must communicate with clarity and confidence for the adult to understand what they are being taught.

TO FEEL GOOD, I NEED...

⋙⎯♡⎯▷ To feel good, I NEED...

_____

_____

_____

_____

_____

⋙⎯♡⎯▷ This is how Mom and Dad help me to feel good...

_____

_____

_____

_____

⋙⎯♡⎯▷ To feel even better, I need Mom and Dad to...

_____

_____

_____

_____

22

■

TO FEEL GOOD I NEED…

What do you need to feel good?
How do Mom and Dad help you to feel better?
What do you need Mom and Dad to do for you to feel
even better?

Instructions for parents: In the first question, guide your child to think of an answer that does not focus on material objects and that depends, entirely or mostly, on the child themself. For example, thinking of something good that happened to me today, giving Mom or Dad a hug, playing in the park, etc.

For the second and third questions, let the child speak without interrupting and without judgment. When they finished, help them to revise and change answers that are not aligned with the goal of the exercise (when the child asks for something that doesn't depend on the parents, or is a material object, or is something that's not good for them, etc.). It's not about eliminating but rather replacing an answer with one that elicits the same feeling in the child (to feel good).

Goal: The child learns to identify their well-being needs. They learn to ask for what they need from their parents in a healthy way.

■ ★

23

I'M NOT AFRAID TO SAY NO

There was a forest where many animals lived. One day, the most playful of the animals, a doe named Luna, wanted to play with someone, but they all rejected her.

The rabbit hid behind a tree and then ran away without saying anything to the doe.
"What's wrong with him?" thought the doe.
The wolf got angry and wanted to attack Luna. He yelled at her to leave him alone and continued taking his nap. "Why is he so angry?» wondered Luna. **The owl** didn't want to play with her either. He told her, calmly and confidently, that he didn't feel like playing now. Luna understood and finally went to play alone.

Which of the 3 animals reacted the best? Why? If you had to tell a friend that you don't want to do something, how would you tell them? Would you tell them like the rabbit, the wolf, or the owl? Why?

Instructions for parents: Explain the importance of saying no and the right way to do it, using the example of the owl.

Goal: Sometimes, children get carried away by toxic dynamics or negative influences because they have a hard time rejecting another person. Knowing how to say no assertively and without having to hide or get angry helps the child to defend their own ideas and avoid acting insensitively.

24

■ ★

LET'S MAKE A DEAL

We don't always get what we want when we ask someone for something. But even if they say no, it doesn't mean there is no chance to have what we want. We just need to find a way for both parties to win: we make a deal.

Example: You want to play a board game with your brother, but he prefers to watch the TV. What if you offer a deal? If he plays with you, in exchange, you will make him a cup of that hot chocolate that he likes so much. Let's see if it works!

Instructions for parents: Help your child think of possible deals to put this idea into practice whenever their request is rejected. What deal could they make with family members to get something that they've wanted for a long time? Try to encourage creative ideas of winning deals.

Goal: The child learns that rejection isn't always final and that they can try to negotiate so that all parties win. This exercise increases the child's confidence and offers a more optimistic perspective on rejection. This way, the child understands that only their first attempt has been rejected, but that they have many more attempts to succeed. This exercise also helps the child to empathize with others and to see things from another person's perspective.

CONFIDENCE, OVERCOMING ADVERSITY, AND RESILIENCE

25

■ ★

THE LION AND THE MOUSE

There was a little mouse who, whenever something bad happened to him, would say, "Oh, poor me, only bad things happen to me! This is unfair!" And he kept on crying without doing anything to make himself feel better. But he had a lion friend who, whenever something bad happened to him, would say,

"I cannot have only good things happen to me. Sometimes good things happen, and sometimes bad things happen. But I often find a way to solve problems and, if I can't do it alone, I look for someone to help me."

Questions for the child to understand the moral of this story:

- If the little mouse broke something, what would he do? And what would the lion do?
- If the little mouse was afraid, what would he do? What would the lion do?
- The adult should think of a question along these lines but adapted to the child's needs.

Instructions for parents: Think of more examples of things that happen or frequently happen to your child, which your child doesn't know how to handle. Ask what the little mouse and the lion would do.

Goal: The child can understand that it's normal for bad things to happen sometimes, but what counts is their response to the situation. The little mouse takes the approach of victimizing themself and reinforcing their low self-esteem. In contrast, the lion assumes responsibility and manages the situation with self-esteem and confidence, asking for help when necessary.

26

★

WE CAN LEARN FROM MISTAKES

When you make a mistake, think:
What have I learned?
What can I do to avoid repeating the same mistake?

We all experience failure at different times, but the
important thing is to learn from it.

Instructions for parents: This is a good exercise for situations when a child feels bad after making a mistake. To create a space of confidence and empathy, you can share your own mistakes with the child and answer the same questions.

Goal: The child understands that mistakes are a part of life and learns to manage them practically, without feeling paralyzed by guilt.

27

★

I DESERVE IT

What good things do you think you don't deserve?
Why?

Instructions for parents: Ask questions to understand why your child doesn't feel worthy of something and identify whether they are connecting an event with the sense of unworthiness. Explain things clearly to them.

Example:

- A child thinks that she doesn't deserve the gift she asks for. It's an expensive object, and her parents don't want to (or can't) buy it. Her parents should explain to her that the fact that she is not receiving the gift is unrelated to her being deserving or undeserving. Her parents should think of an alternate gift that also excites her and tell her that she'll receive it when it's time (birthday, Christmas, etc.), or offer something that is non-material in nature to replace the gift (going to a theme park, an interesting museum, a magic show, etc.). Reinforce ideas such as "you don't need material things to be happy", "money can't buy happiness", "you deserve good things in life, and if you look for them, you'll find them".

- A child thinks he doesn't deserve to have a lot of friends at school. Ask questions to understand what's happening in his life that is making him feel that way. Reinforce ideas like "when you love yourself, you love the world more, and the world loves you more".

Goal: Recognize when a child has started to associate an event with a sense of not being deserving. Explain to the child that whether or not they receive a gift is not related to whether they are deserving of the gift or are worthy as a person.

IF THEY CRITICIZE ME, I DO THIS

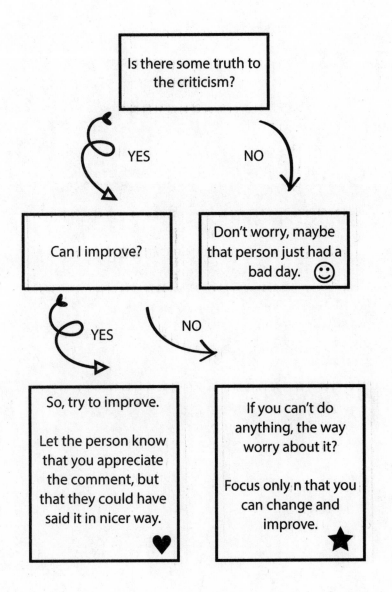

Is there some truth to the criticism?

YES   NO

Can I improve?

Don't worry, maybe that person just had a bad day. 😊

YES   NO

So, try to improve.

Let the person know that you appreciate the comment, but that they could have said it in nicer way. ♥

If you can't do anything, the way worry about it?

Focus only n that you can change and improve. ★

28

★

RESPONDING TO CRITICISM

When someone criticizes you, ask yourself the questions that appear on the previous page.

Example 1: My friend has told me that I always arrive late. Is this true? No.

Example 2: A classmate mocks me because I'm small. Is this true? Yes. Can I do something about it? No. Can I make the situation better? Yes. I ask the classmate to please stop making fun of me. If that doesn't help, I talk to a teacher or my parents and explain what's happening.

Example 3: Mom or Dad have scolded me because my room is always messy. Is this true? Yes. Can I do something to make it better? Yes.

Instructions for parents: Help your child to understand criticism, based on examples from real life, or practice using hypothetical examples. When criticism is based on facts, and the child concludes that they can improve, you can help them to see **how** to face that situation.

Goal: The child learns to distinguish constructive from non-constructive criticism and to act accordingly. By understanding that not all criticism is well-founded, the child learns to not take it personally.

I DON'T KNOW WHAT TO DO
(MAKING DECISIONS)

What would my hero do?

_____

_____

_____

_____

_____

What would Mom, Dad, or an adult with a lot of experience do?

_____

_____

_____

_____

_____

What would I like to do?

_____

_____

_____

_____

_____

29

★

I DON'T KNOW WHAT TO DO

Sometimes we don't know what to do or what decision to make. This happens to everybody.
When you have doubts about how to decide, ask yourself these questions:

Part 1:

What would my hero or someone good do? (Consult exercise 17)
What would Mom, Dad, or an adult with a lot of experience do?
What would I like to do?

Part 2:

The right decision always considers these three things:
what you like, what's smart, and what's good and correct.
Think of decisions that you've already made in your life where these three points were satisfied compared to others where they weren't, and explain what happened.

Instructions for parents: This exercise can be done with small children (Part 1), as well as older children (Parts 1 and 2). Based on the age of the child, it is recommended that parents adapt the questions and determine the extent to which they should interfere or advise. For older kids, this provides good decision-making practice, and it is better to intervene less so that the child can make decisions on their own (as long as it's a decision that they have the ability and authority to make).

Goal: The child learns to put themself in the shoes of someone they admire, someone with more experience, etc., to see the issue from a more mature perspective and learn how to make better decisions.

30

■

DUTY AND PLEASURE

We cannot just enjoy every day and play without
having any duties or responsibilities.
We also cannot only have duties every day without
experiencing any pleasure.
The secret to happiness lies in balance.

What duties did you have today?
(Think about homework, chores, something that you
had to do, even if you didn't
feel like it).

What pleasures did you experience today?
(Think about games, TV, gifts, some or sweets you
ate today).

Do you think that you had a good balance today?
Why?

Instructions for parents: Help your child to identify their duties
and pleasures. Remind them of the joys they experienced, which
they may have ignored or forgotten (we tend to remember obli-
gations more than pleasures). Analyze together whether there
was a healthy balance.

Goal: For a child to develop into a healthy and mature adult, it is necessary to learn to balance responsibilities and pleasures. A child that doesn't learn to consider duties as a part of their day can be more prone to developing a low tolerance to frustration and to be discontent. A child that doesn't learn to reward or enjoy themself may end up having low self-esteem. The goal of this exercise is to help the child to find a healthy balance to develop strong and mature self-esteem.

31

★

I WILL TRY!

There was a boy who was scared of going down to
the basement of his house.
"What if there's a monster? Or a big spider?"
he thought.
One day his dad accompanied him and showed him
there wasn't anything
dangerous in the basement.
From that day on, the child went down alone and
without fear, because
there was nothing to be worried about!

Is there something that you're scared of doing? It must
be an activity (for example, swimming, riding a bike,
going shopping alone, or sleeping outside of the
home).

Who can help you to overcome this fear?
Try to do one thing that scares you but isn't really
dangerous.
You will see that it isn't so bad!

Instructions for parents: Help the child to identify their fears
and support them to overcome them, starting with small steps.

For example, the fear of petting a dog. Think of a friend that has a good dog and organize a meeting where the child first observes the dog from a distance, then gets a little closer, etc. Take it step-by-step until they get over their fear.

Goal: The child overcomes their fear by carefully exposing themself to the source of their fear, at their own pace and supported by their parents, gaining confidence that fears can be overcome.

SUCCESS STARTS WITH A GOOD PLAN

I want to achieve: _____

Step 1 _____

When do I do it? _____

Step 2 _____

When do I do it? _____

Step 3 _____

When do I do it? _____

32

■ ★

SUCCESS STARTS WITH
A GOOD PLAN

What would you like to achieve?
If you want to achieve something difficult, first you will
need a good plan.

Write down a goal you want to achieve on the
previous page and think of 3 steps you need to take to
achieve this goal.

When you take the first step, you can color in the
first pair of feet. With the second step completed,
color the second pair of feet. You're already one
step closer to your goal! Color in the third and last
step when you achieved your goal.
Congratulations!

Instructions for parents: It's better for the child to note
goals that can be achieved in the **short term** and that are
realistic. This will make the goal more motivating and tangible for the child.

Example: Learning how to count to 100 in another language. Make sure that the child's goals are not overly challenging or too focused on the long-term (e.g., "I want to be a doctor").

Goal: The child learns that it's easier to achieve a goal when it's clearly identified, divided into parts or steps, and a plan is developed. In this way, the goal seems closer and this encourages the child more, because it will be more realistic to achieve.

EXERCISE TABLE

#	EXERCISE	TYPE	WHEN TO DO THE EXERCISE
4	I'M AFRAID OF…		Fear of something.
9	I AM CAPABLE		Lack of confidence to do or, achieve something.
17	MY SUPERHERO		Lack of confidence, discomfort or, insecurity.
19	MY FAVORITE ANIMAL		Lack of confidence, discomfort or, insecurity.
26	WE CAN LEARN FROM MISTAKES		Making a mistake.
27	I DESERVE IT		Sense of not deserving something.
28	RESPONDING TO CRITICISM		Facing criticism or, teasing.
29	I DON'T KNOW WHAT TO DO		Doubts, problems making decisions, or, choices.

31	I WILL TRY!		Fear of doing something, fear of the unknown.
2	A TIGER DOESN'T WANT TO HAVE WINGS		On a monthly basis/ comparison to others.
6	THE EMOTIONS GAME		Practice frequently to be conscious of emotions/the presence of a negative emotion.
7	WHAT DO I SEE IN THE MIRROR?		To develop a positive self-image of the body and recognize shame or discomfort with a body part.
11	I AM ME		Practice frequently/ comparison to others.
12	INVISIBLE GIFTS		Practice frequently/ before sleeping/ moments of frustration and anger.
13	I CAN TURN IT AROUND!		Practice frequently/ moments of frustration and negativity.

16	HAPPY HERE AND NOW		Practice frequently/ before sleeping/ moments of frustration and anger.
18	GOOD FRIENDS		Practice frequently/ problems in friendships.
20	TOGETHER WE ACCOMPLISH MORE		Practice frequently/ ask for help.
23	I'M NOT AFRAID TO SAY "NO"		Practice frequently/ trouble saying "NO".
24	LET'S MAKE A DEAL		Practice frequently/ facing rejection.
25	THE LION AND THE MOUSE		Practice frequently/ victimization.
32	SUCCESS STARTS WITH A GOOD PLAN		On monthly basis/to achieve something.
1	I AM BRAVE		Practice frequently.
3	I LEARN A LOT OF THINGS		Practice frequently.
5	MY SUPER POWER		Practice frequently.

8	THE POWER OF MY HABITS		Practice frequently.
10	MY STRENGTHS		Practice frequently.
14	MY LIST OF DREAMS		Write once and check every once in a while.
15	WHAT WOULD I DO WITHOUT?		Practice frequently.
21	TODAY I WILL TEACH YOU SOMETHING		On a monthly basis.
22	TO FEEL GOOD, I NEED…		Practice frequently.
30	DUTY AND PLEASURE		Practice frequently/ before sleeping/ moments of anger and frustration.

COPIES OF DRAWINGS AND EXERCISES

Cover Drawing

WHAT HAVE I LEARNED?

My new KNOWLEDGE is...

_____

_____

_____

_____

_____

My new ABILITIES are...

_____

_____

_____

_____

From my EXPERIENCE, I have learned that...

_____

_____

_____

_____

MY SUPERPOWER

My SUPERPOWER is…

_____

_____

_____

_____

_____

I use this SUPERPOWER when…

_____

_____

_____

_____

The best thing about my SUPERPOWER is…

_____

_____

_____

_____

THE EMOTIONS GAME

HAPPY

SCARED

GRATEFUL

WORRIED

EXCITED

ANGRY

KIND

BORED

FRUSTRATED

CONFUSED

STRESSED

CALM

LONELY

FEELING INJUSTICE

ANXIOUS

CONFIDENT

GUILTY

ENVIOUS

BRAVE

CHEERFUL

CURIOUS

ASHAMED

SAD

GLAD

THRILLED

THE POWER OF MY HABITS

My GOOD habits are…

_____

_____

_____

_____

_____

My BAD habits are…

_____

_____

_____

_____

_____

What other good habits could I include in my list and practice?
Today I can switch a bad habit for a good one, which one will
it be?

_____

_____

_____

_____

_____

MY STRENGTHS

Strengths that I see in me...

_____

_____

_____

_____

_____

Strengths that OTHERS see in me...

_____

_____

_____

_____

_____

My 3 FAVORITE strengths are...

Strength 1 _____

_____

Strength 2 _____

_____

Strength 3 _____

_____

MY LIST OF DREAMS

Dream 1: _____

_____

_____

☆ ☆ ☆

Dream 2: _____

_____

_____

☆ ☆ ☆

Dream 3: _____

_____

_____

☆ ☆ ☆

HAPPY HERE AND NOW

These are 5 things that make me happy here and now:

1. _____

2. _____

3. _____

4. _____

5. _____

DRAW YOUR SUPERHERO

MY SUPERHERO IS:

_____

DRAW YOUR FAVORITE ANIMAL:

MY FAVORITE ANIMAL IS:

_____

TO FEEL GOOD, I NEED...

➤♡➤ To feel good, I NEED...

_____

_____

_____

_____

_____

➤♡➤ This is how Mom and Dad help me to feel good...

_____

_____

_____

_____

➤♡➤ To feel even better, I need Mom and Dad to...

_____

_____

_____

_____

IF THEY CRITICIZE ME, I DO THIS

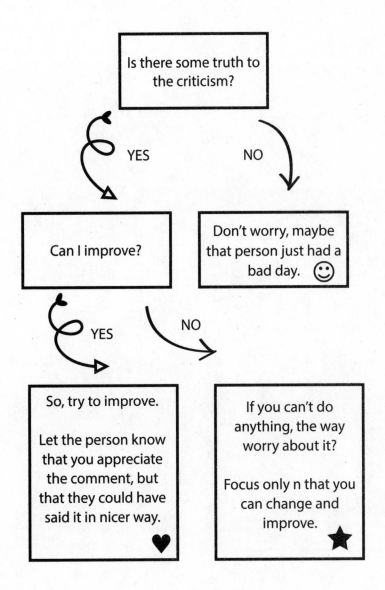

Is there some truth to the criticism?

YES

NO

Can I improve?

Don't worry, maybe that person just had a bad day. ☺

YES

NO

So, try to improve.

Let the person know that you appreciate the comment, but that they could have said it in nicer way. ♥

If you can't do anything, the way worry about it?

Focus only n that you can change and improve. ★

I DON'T KNOW WHAT TO DO
(MAKING DECISIONS)

What would my hero do?

_____

_____

_____

_____

_____

What would Mom, Dad, or an adult with a lot of experience do?

_____

_____

_____

_____

_____

What would I like to do?

_____

_____

_____

_____

_____

SUCCESS STARTS WITH A GOOD PLAN

I want to achieve: _____

Step 1 _____

_____

When do I do it? _____

Step 2 _____

_____

When do I do it? _____

Step 3 _____

_____

When do I do it? _____

Thank you so much for buying this book.

Thank you, in advance, for your time.

Jana Capri and Charan Díaz